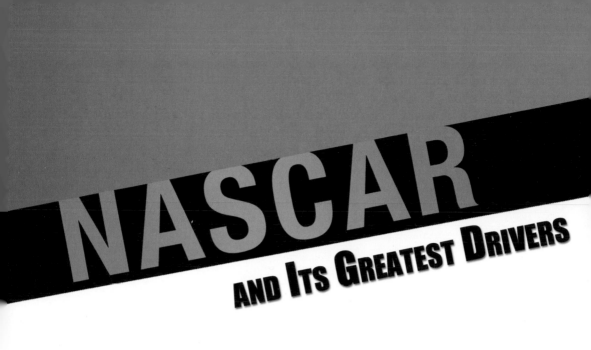

NASCAR

AND ITS GREATEST DRIVERS

inside sports

NASCAR
AND ITS GREATEST DRIVERS

EDITED BY NATALIE REGIS

Britannica®
Educational Publishing
IN ASSOCIATION WITH

ROSEN
EDUCATIONAL SERVICES

Published in 2015 by Britannica Educational Publishing (a trademark of Encyclopædia Britannica, Inc.) in association with The Rosen Publishing Group, Inc.
29 East 21st Street, New York, NY 10010

Distributed exclusively by Rosen Publishing.
To see additional Britannica Educational Publishing titles, go to rosenpublishing.com.

First Edition

Britannica Educational Publishing
J. E. Luebering: Director, Core Reference Group
Anthony L. Green: Editor, Compton's by Britannica

Rosen Publishing
Hope Lourie Killcoyne: Executive Editor
Natalie Regis: Editor
Nelson Sá: Art Director
Nicole Russo: Designer
Cindy Reiman: Photography Manager

Library of Congress Cataloging-in-Publication Data

NASCAR and its greatest drivers/edited by Natalie Regis.
       pages cm.—(Inside sports)
Includes bibliographical references and index.
ISBN 978-1-62275-590-5 (library bound)
1. Stock car racing—Juvenile literature. 2. Automobile racing drivers—Juvenile literature. 3. NASCAR (Association)—Juvenile literature. I. Regis, Natalie, editor of compilation.
GV1029.9.S74N3755 2015
796.72—dc23
                                                                 2014022805

Manufactured in the United States of America

On the cover, page 3: Jimmie Johnson. *Robert Duyos/Sun Sentinel/Tribune News Service/Getty Images*

Interior pages background image EPG EuroPhotoGraphics/Shutterstock.com; Silhouettes © iStockphoto.com/Big Ryan, © iStockphoto.com/artpro63; back cover, pp. 71–80 baranq/Shutterstock.com.

CONTENTS

INTRODUCTION

The thrill of a NASCAR race starts long before the green flag waves. With the sight of the colorful cars, the sound of the engines starting up, and the smell of tires burning on the asphalt, fans and drivers alike experience pure adrenaline from beginning to end.

Soon the drivers are introduced individually. They wave to the crowd as they walk across the track, and then they crawl into the windows of their cars. The crowd stands up to cheer, yell, clap their hands, and whistle for their favorite driver. Race time is close.

Finally, there is the announcement "Drivers, start your engines!" The air is filled with the sound of dozens of roaring, revving engines. The pace car leads the NASCAR drivers out, giving them a chance to warm up. Then the pace car pulls over and the green

Brad Keselowski (right) and Jimmie Johnson (left) lead a Sprint Cup race in November 2012. Beelde Photography/Shutterstock.com

flag is waved. The race has begun! Cars speed up, engines scream, and the track is full of skilled drivers jockeying for the lead.

This volume is a look into the history of NASCAR, its rules, and its most famous drivers. It has everything a fan needs to know about NASCAR—the fastest, most exciting race in the U.S.A.

CHAPTER 1

NASCAR Then and Now

From its humble beginnings on the beaches of Florida, NASCAR racing has grown to become one of the most popular spectator sports in the United States. NASCAR—in full, the National Association for Stock Car Auto Racing—is the premier organization in American stock-car racing, which today features purpose-built race cars that outwardly resemble standard-model cars. It's a far cry from the sport's early days, when drivers might race a car they drove to the track.

NASCAR's Beginnings

Stock-car racing is said to have originated during the Prohibition period (1919–33), when the manufacture, transportation, and sale of alcoholic beverages was outlawed in the United States. Illegal still operators, needing cars capable of more than ordinary speed to

Car racing has a long history, beginning with the first gas-powered automobiles. Fox Photos/Hulton Archive/Getty Images

evade the law while transporting liquor, tuned and altered ordinary passenger automobiles to make them faster. After the end of Prohibition, these cars were raced for pleasure, particularly in the southeastern states.

Stock-car racing became popular on the shores of Daytona Beach, Fla., in the 1930s. The key figure on the Daytona racing scene was Bill France, an auto mechanic and sometime race-car driver who organized stock-car races on the beach throughout the 1930s and '40s. In 1947, after several unsuccessful attempts to create a series of races that would determine a national champion, France created the National Championship Stock Car Circuit (NCSCC), a yearlong series of 40 races held across the southeastern United States. France was responsible

Bill France Sr, NASCAR's founder and first president, walks down the Daytona International Speedway in 1968. **Eric Schweikardt/Sports Illustrated/Getty Images**

for establishing and enforcing the technical regulations that governed the cars, and he created a scoring system that would award drivers points used to determine a series champion. He also organized and promoted each race and awarded cash prizes to the winners of races and to the series champion.

Although the NCSCC was successful, France had greater ambitions. He organized a series of meetings in December 1947 with the goal of establishing a still-larger stock-car-racing series. What emerged from those meetings was NASCAR, which replaced the NCSCC. France was its first president. The first NASCAR race was held on January 4, 1948, in Pompano Beach, Florida. In February of that year NASCAR was incorporated, with France the primary stockholder.

In 1949, NASCAR changed the rules governing the cars. Up to that time, "modifieds"—cars varying in age and in the mechanical modifications made to them for the purpose of racing—were allowed to compete. Starting in June 1949, however, only late-model (recently manufactured) stock cars were permitted. Races that year were called Strictly Stock races, and Red Byron became the series champion.

NOTABLE WOMEN OF NASCAR'S EARLY DAYS

SARA CHRISTIAN

Sara Christian (1918–1980) finished 14th of 33 drivers in NASCAR's first Strictly Stock race, held in Charlotte, N.C., on June 19, 1949. She also took part in six other races in 1949–50, earning two top-10 finishes. She was voted "Woman Driver of the Year" in 1949.

ETHEL FLOCK MOBLEY

Ethel Flock Mobley (1920–1984) participated in two Strictly Stock races in 1949. In the Daytona

Ethel Flock Mobley was named after ethyl, the type of gas her father used in his taxi. **RacingOne/ISC Archives/Getty Images**

Beach race on July 10, she competed against her three brothers, Tim, Fonty, and Bob, defeating two of them. It was the only NASCAR event to feature four siblings. Mobley also competed in many all-women races.

LOUISE SMITH

Louise Smith (1916–2006) got her start outrunning the police in her native South Carolina. Nicknamed the Good Ol' Gal by her fellow racers, Smith competed in 11 Strictly Stock and Grand National races between 1949 and 1952, with four top-20 finishes. She was the first woman inducted into the International Motorsports Hall of Fame

RISE TO NATIONAL PROMINENCE

France changed the name of the series to Grand National in 1950. That name was used until 1971, when the tobacco company R.J. Reynolds bought sponsorship rights to the series and renamed it the Winston Cup Series (it was also known as the Cup Series or NASCAR Cup Series). By then, stock cars were built specifically for racing. NASCAR's rules required cars to resemble their stock counterparts in their dimensions and appearance, but car owners, drivers, and mechanics increasingly

Bill France Jr. (right), *succeeded his father as president of NASCAR in 1972.* **RacingOne/ISC Archives/Getty Images**

exploited those rules in their attempts to gain a competitive advantage. NASCAR was also responsible for requiring equipment in cars that, by 1970, had reached over 200 miles (322 kilometers) per hour in nonrace conditions.

In the 1970s, there was an expansion of corporate advertising, which was both a function of and spur to NASCAR's growing national profile. NASCAR itself underwent a number of changes, with France stepping down as president in 1972 in favor of Bill France, Jr., his son. After years of experimenting with the number of points awarded for each race, NASCAR in 1975 imposed a scoring system that remained in place until 2004, thereby inaugurating the "modern era" of the Cup Series. The 1970s were dominated by Richard Petty and Cale Yarborough, who between them won eight championships from 1971 to 1980.

In the 1980s, Darrell Waltrip and Dale Earnhardt emerged as the most prominent drivers in the Cup Series. The sport continued to expand, and in 1984 Ronald Reagan became the first sitting U.S. president to attend a Cup Series race. In the 1990s, Earnhardt won four championships and Jeff Gordon won three. In 1994, the Indianapolis Motor Speedway, the home of the Indianapolis 500, hosted its first Cup Series race.

Rescue workers arrive after Dale Earnhardt's crash in the last lap of the Daytona 500 in 2001. Marc Serota/Hulton Archive/Getty Images

NASCAR IN THE 21ST CENTURY

In February 2001, Earnhardt was killed in a last-lap crash during the Daytona 500. Driver safety became a high-profile concern, and NASCAR implemented a number of measures intended to increase safety at racetracks.

Other changes to the Cup Series during the first decade of the 21st century included the naming of Brian France as his father's successor as head of NASCAR in 2003 and experimentation with several scoring systems intended to increase competition at the end of the season. The building of new racetracks outside Chicago and Kansas City, Kans., continued efforts begun by NASCAR in the 1990s to expand beyond the southeast United States, its traditional base. After the phone company Nextel announced it would succeed R.J. Reynolds as the series sponsor, the Winston Cup Series was renamed in 2004 the Nextel Cup Series. In 2008, the series name changed again, to the Sprint Cup Series. In 2007, the Japanese automaker Toyota entered the Cup Series, traditionally dominated by American manufacturers. By the end of the first decade of the 21st century, Jimmie Johnson had emerged as the dominant driver in the Cup Series. In 2010, he became the first driver to win five consecutive series championships.

In addition to overseeing the Cup Series, NASCAR sanctions two other major national series. The Nationwide Series, founded in 1982 and called the Busch Series from 1984 to 2007, features race cars that differ somewhat in engine and body size from Cup cars. The Camping World Truck Series, founded as the Super Truck Series in 1995 and called the Craftsman Truck Series from 1996 to 2008, features race cars with bodies like those of pickup

CARS IN THE MOVIES

Throw together a NASCAR track and a few famous actors and what do you get? Chances are, a great movie.

Car races have been a popular part of movies for decades. Since the 1960s, movies have featured race-car drivers who compete in NASCAR races. From Elvis Presley in 1968's *Speedway* and Tom Cruise in 1990's *Days of Thunder* to Will Ferrell in 2006's *Talladega Nights: The Ballad of Ricky Bobby*, big stars have gotten behind the wheel in movies that show race-car driving up close and personal.

NASCAR racing earned countless young fans when Pixar released *Cars* in 2006. This time the cars were the characters, with a first-time racer named Lightning McQueen competing to win the Piston Cup. The movie was so popular that a sequel was made in 2011. This time Lightning McQueen headed overseas to compete in the World Grand Prix.

A promotional poster from *Cars 2*, featuring Lightning McQueen. © Walt Disney/courtesy Everett Collection

18

trucks. NASCAR also sanctions a number of regional series in the United States.

THE DAYTONA 500

In the mid-1950s, observing the success of tracks such as Darlington Raceway in South Carolina, Bill France built a track at Daytona Beach large enough to host NASCAR races. Daytona International Speedway hosted its first Daytona 500 in 1959, and over the following years the 500 became the most prestigious

Drivers Fred Lorenzen (#28) and Ned Jarrett (#11) race in the Daytona 500 in February 1963. **Michael Rougier/The LIFE Picture Collection/ Getty Images**

event in the NASCAR season, as well as one of the world's preeminent racing events. The "500" in the name refers to the number of miles drivers race—200 laps around a 2.5 mile (4 km) tri-oval track.

In the early 21st century, as NASCAR exploded in popularity, the Daytona 500 became one of the best-attended and highest-rated sporting events in the United States. Prominent drivers who have won at Daytona include Richard Petty (whose father, Lee, won the first race in 1959), Cale Yarborough, Jeff Gordon, and Dale Earnhardt, who died after a crash in the 2001 race.

NASCAR CHAMPIONS

YEAR	WINNER	YEAR	WINNER
1949	R. Byron	1958	L. Petty
1950	B. Rexford	1959	L. Petty
1951	H. Thomas	1960	R. White
1952	T. Flock	1961	N. Jarrett
1953	H. Thomas	1962	J. Weatherly
1954	L. Petty	1963	J. Weatherly
1955	T. Flock	1964	R. Petty
1956	B. Baker	1965	N. Jarrett
1957	B. Baker	1966	D. Pearson

YEAR	WINNER	YEAR	WINNER
1967	R. Petty	1993	D. Earnhardt
1968	D. Pearson	1994	D. Earnhardt
1969	D. Pearson	1995	J. Gordon
1970	B. Isaac	1996	T. Labonte
1971	R. Petty	1997	J. Gordon
1972	R. Petty	1998	J. Gordon
1973	B. Parsons	1999	D. Jarrett
1974	R. Petty	2000	B. Labonte
1975	R. Petty	2001	J. Gordon
1976	C. Yarborough	2002	T. Stewart
1977	C. Yarborough	2003	M. Kenseth
1978	C. Yarborough	2004	K. Busch
1979	R. Petty	2005	T. Stewart
1980	D. Earnhardt	2006	J. Johnson
1981	D. Waltrip	2007	J. Johnson
1982	D. Waltrip	2008	J. Johnson
1983	B. Allison	2009	J. Johnson
1984	T. Labonte	2010	J. Johnson
1985	D. Waltrip	2011	T. Stewart
1986	D. Earnhardt	2012	B. Keselowski
1987	D. Earnhardt	2013	J. Johnson
1988	B. Elliott	2014	K. Harvick
1989	R. Wallace		
1990	D. Earnhardt		
1991	D. Earnhardt		
1992	A. Kulwicki		

CHAPTER 2

RACING RULES

Each year NASCAR issues a lengthy book detailing the rules of the sport, from approved cars and equipment to race procedures and scoring. Though the scoring rules are shared with everyone, only people in the "inner circle" of NASCAR get to look inside the rule book.

CAR REQUIREMENTS

Cars used in NASCAR races are modified versions of standard cars. The NASCAR rule book specifies the models that are allowed in competition. As of the 2014 season, the three approved models for Sprint Cup races were the Chevrolet SS, the Ford Fusion, and the Toyota Camry. All body panels except the rear deck lid are made by the manufacturer and are stamped for verification.

A street car and its NASCAR version are still quite different, however. NASCAR cars

Kyle Busch drives in the NASCAR Kobalt 400 in Las Vegas, Nev., in 2013.
Beelde Photography/Shutterstock.com

have a number of special safety features to protect the driver in the event of a crash. One of the most important safety enhancements is the roll cage, a framework of metal bars designed to keep the driver from being crushed if the car rolls over. Stock cars are also lower to the ground than their street counterparts and have tires with no tread, or grooves, which gives them a better grip on the track.

Teams can make modifications to various components of their cars. However, NASCAR has strict rules about equipment to ensure that

FLAG RULES

The chart below shows how flags are used in NASCAR.

Start/Restart		Return to pits for a penalty/mechanical problem
Caution		Driver no longer scored for failing to pit
Debris on track/Slippery track		Course partially blocked
Pit road closed		Faster car approaching
Final lap		Race completed

During a race, drivers and their pit crew are required to pay attention to the flags, which can indicate both safety and race information. **Jon Feingerish/Stone/Getty Images**

one car doesn't have an unfair advantage over others. For example, all Sprint Cup cars must weigh a minimum of 3,300 pounds (1,497 kg) and have an eight cylinder, fuel-injected engine. Some requirements are track specific, such as the removal of all side windows on tracks less than 1 1/3 miles (2.15 km) in length. Any adjustments made to the body of a car must conform to numerous templates provided by NASCAR. Cars are thoroughly inspected to ensure that the rules are followed. An illegal modification could mean losing points or a fine.

QUALIFYING PROCEDURES

Before every NASCAR race, the cars go through a qualifying procedure to determine

The Talladega Superspeedway in Alabama hosts a Sprint Cup race.
Education Images/Universal Images Group/Getty Images

the order in which they line up at the starting line of the race. The drivers who perform best in the qualifying rounds get the best starting positions. The best position of all is called the pole position.

NATIONAL SERIES

NASCAR changed the qualifying procedures for its three national series—the Sprint Cup, the Nationwide Series, and the Camping World Truck Series—beginning with the 2014 season. Single-car runs were replaced with a group qualifying format.

The qualifying procedure depends on the length of the track. For tracks that measure less than 1.25 miles (2 km), as well as road courses, qualifying consists of two rounds. The first round is 30 minutes long. The 12 cars that complete one lap the fastest advance to the next round, which lasts 10 minutes. Starting positions are assigned in order based on qualifying times.

At tracks measuring 1.25 miles (2 km) or longer, qualifying requires three rounds. The first round is 25 minutes long, and the 24 cars with the fastest single-lap times advance to the second round. The second round is 10 minutes, and the 12 fastest cars advance to the 5-minute third round. The car with the best time in the third round earns the pole position.

Regardless of the size of the track, all cars must follow a number of rules in the qualifying rounds, For example, cars may complete as many laps as possible during the allotted time, but they can enter and exit the track only when the green flag is displayed. Other

Qualifying rounds determine drivers' starting positions in a race. A good starting position can be a big advantage. **Jon Feingerish/ Stone/Getty Images**

qualifying rules state that timed laps cannot begin or end on pit roads and that only one set of tires may be used.

DAYTONA 500

Though the Daytona 500 is part of the Sprint Cup, its qualifying rules are quite different from the other Cup races. The process begins a week before the race, when drivers complete two laps in single-car runs. The faster of the two laps is the driver's qualifying time. The two fastest drivers earn the top two starting spots in

Trucks compete in the Mudsummer Classic, a popular event in NASCAR's Camping World Truck Series. **Chris Graythen/NASCAR/ Getty Images**

the 500. A few days later all the drivers participate in one of two 150-mile (241 km) qualifying races. These races determine all of the starting positions after the top two.

MUDSUMMER CLASSIC

The Mudsummer Classic, held at Eldora Speedway in Rossburg, Ohio, is another race with unique qualifying rules. Part of the Camping World Truck Series, this race features pickup trucks driving on a dirt track. Single-truck qualifying runs determine starting positions in five qualifying races. Five trucks from each of the five qualifying races earn a place in the Mudsummer Classic. The remaining trucks can compete in the Last Chance Race, with the top four finishers making it to the Mudsummer Classic. The 30th and final spot in the Classic goes either to the most recent series champion or to the next highest finisher in the Last Chance Race.

DRIVER SAFETY

NASCAR fans have never denied that part of the attraction of their favorite sport is the element of danger. The skill of the drivers, the talent of the car constructors, and

Colin Braun (#16), Steve Wallace (#66), and Brian Scott (#11) crash in a 2010 race. Braun and Wallace had to leave the race, but Scott was able to continue. **Action Sports Photography/Shutterstock.com**

the rules of the race were designed to balance the danger and thus maintain the element of exciting competition. In 2000–01, that balance was sorely tested by four deaths within nine months in NASCAR events. Among those killed was Dale Earnhardt—one of the icons of the sport—during the Daytona 500.

Earnhardt's death forced NASCAR to get serious about safety. Since then, the organization has introduced many new safety rules about vehicle construction, driver clothing, the manner of racing, and the conditions on the track. Newly designed protective seats and improved belt systems were built into cars. NASCAR also began developing a race car called the Car of Tomorrow, which included crushable materials and other features designed to provide the driver with greater protection during a crash. The Car of Tomorrow was used in about half of the races during the 2007 season and was adopted for the full season in 2008, and the safety innovations developed then were adopted in subsequent generations of race cars. NASCAR tracks were made safer by the installation of "soft walls"—steel-and-foam barriers that are intended to absorb the energy of a crash.

Earnhardt died of a skull fracture caused by movement of the head during his crash. In 2002, in an effort to prevent this type of injury, NASCAR made head-and-neck restraint devices a requirement for its drivers. By far the most popular choice among drivers is the HANS (head and neck support) device. It was developed in the early 1980s by engineer Robert Hubbard and former racing champion Jim Downing. The device allows normal movement of the head and neck but limits the extreme front-to-back and side-to-side

The cockpit of a NASCAR car features a number of advanced safety features to protect the driver. **Michael Krinke/E+/Getty Images**

movements that could make a crash fatal. In 2007, a second head restraint—the Hutchens hybrid device—was approved, though most drivers continued to use HANS.

In 2003, NASCAR opened a research and development facility in Concord, N.C., to develop new technology for race cars and safety equipment. The facility also is home to an accident investigation group, which analyzes data recorded by the crash recorder boxes installed in each car.

CHAPTER 3

NASCAR LEGENDS

Becoming a NASCAR driver demands a combination of hand-and-eye coordination, physical dexterity, and a competitive spirit. You have to have total confidence in your ability to handle pressure and make fast but wise decisions. While many people have climbed behind the wheel of a NASCAR race car, only a few have become true legends.

BOBBY ALLISON

Bobby Allison was one of the most successful drivers in NASCAR history and a member of one of the most notable, and most tragic, families in racing. He raced competitively at NASCAR's highest level for a quarter century.

Robert Arthur Allison was born in Miami, Fla., on Dec. 3, 1937. He took up racing in high school against the wishes of his parents.

Bobby Allison, (left) with his son Davey Allison at the Daytona International Speedway in 1988. **Robert Alexander/Archive Photos/Getty Images**

After making his way to Alabama, Allison, his brother Donnie, and friend Red Farmer formed the roots of the "Alabama Gang," a group of drivers that operated out of a shop near Birmingham.

Allison stepped up to the Grand National (now Sprint Cup) Series in 1965 and achieved his first victory in 1966. Although he only won a single championship, his 84 race victories placed him third on NASCAR's all-time list at the time of his retirement. He also won the Daytona 500 three times (1978, 1982, and 1988).

Allison was involved in key moments in NASCAR history. He was a part of the fight between Donnie Allison and Cale Yarborough at the end of the 1979 Daytona 500, which, through its live-television broadcast in the United States, helped catapult the sport to national prominence. In 1987, his car went airborne at Talladega Speedway in Alabama and tore off a long swath of fencing, injuring many spectators. In response NASCAR mandated that racers use restrictor plates — devices that, by restricting an engine's air intake, limit a car's horsepower and speed — on its superspeedways (Talladega and Daytona).

One year after the Talladega incident, Allison suffered a career-ending wreck at

Pocono Raceway in Pennsylvania. In 1993, both of his sons died in separate accidents— Clifford in a practice accident in Michigan and Davey in a helicopter crash at Talladega.

Allison served as a race-car owner for several years in the 1990s with little success. He was inducted into the NASCAR Hall of Fame in 2011.

MARIO ANDRETTI

Mario Andretti was the first driver to win the Indianapolis 500, the Daytona 500, and the Formula One world championship. During his 30-year career, he won four United States Auto Club (USAC) championships and 52 Championship Auto Racing Teams (CART) races.

Mario Gabriel Andretti and his twin, Aldo, were born on Feb. 28, 1940, in Montona, Italy. The two studied automobile mechanics, frequented racing-car garages, and participated in a race-driver training program in Italy. The family lived in a refugee camp for seven years after World War II before moving to the United States in 1955 and settling in Nazareth, Pa.

By 1958, the brothers were racing stock cars. (After several serious crashes, Aldo retired from racing in 1969.) In the early 1960s, Mario drove sprint and midget cars in races and in 1964 began racing in the championship-car division of the USAC. He won USAC championships in 1965–66, 1969, and 1984. He also won the Daytona 500 stock-car race in 1967 and the sports-car Grand Prix of Endurance race in 1967 and 1970.

Andretti won the Indianapolis 500 race in 1969 with a then-record speed of 156.867 miles (252 km) per hour. His apparent victory in the 1981 race was ultimately given to Bobby Unser due to a penalty for passing cars during a yellow flag. Andretti was the second U.S. driver to win the Formula One world driving championship in 1978. (Phil Hill was the first in 1961.) Andretti retired from competition in 1994. In 1999, a panel of experts in a tie vote named Andretti and A. J. Foyt the best drivers of the century. He was inducted into the International Motorsports Hall of Fame in 2000. Andretti's sons, Jeff and Michael, also became professional race-car drivers.

DALE EARNHARDT

Dale Earnhardt dominated NASCAR during the 1980s and '90s. For much of his career, he was NASCAR's most popular and

Dale Earnhardt Jr. (left) *with Dale Earnhardt Sr. at the Charlotte Motor Speedway, Concord, N.C.* George Tiedemann/Sports Illustrated/Getty Images

controversial driver. He gained a reputation as an aggressive driver and was known as The Intimidator. The sight of his charging number-3 black Chevrolet Monte Carlo rattled many drivers.

Ralph Dale Earnhardt was born on April 29, 1951, in Kannapolis, N.C. His father, Ralph Earnhardt, raced stock cars during the

1960s. The younger Earnhardt dropped out of high school in 1967 to pursue his own interest in racing. In 1975, he made his NASCAR Winston Cup debut at the World 600 in Charlotte, N.C. In 1979, he joined the circuit full-time, earning 17 top-10 finishes and the Rookie of the Year title. In 1980, he raced to 5 victories and 19 top-five finishes, winning his first Winston Cup title. Earnhardt drove to 6 more Winston Cup titles, equaling the career mark of Richard Petty. Despite his success in the series, Earnhardt struggled at NASCAR's premier event, the Daytona 500, where he failed 19 times before receiving the checkered flag in 1998.

Over the course of his driving career, Earnhardt entered 676 Winston Cup races, won 76 of them, and collected more than $40 million in prize money. He was also a four-time winner of the International Race of Champions series (1990, 1995, 1999, 2000).

Earnhardt died on Feb. 18, 2001, from injuries suffered during a crash in the final lap of the Daytona 500. He was inducted into the International Motorsports Hall of Fame in 2006, and he was a member of the inaugural class of the NASCAR Hall of Fame in 2010. His son Dale Jr. also raced in the NASCAR Winston Cup (later Sprint Cup) series.

A. J. FOYT

The only race-car driver to compete in the Indianapolis 500 for 35 consecutive years was A. J. Foyt. He was the first driver to win the prestigious race four times (in 1961, 1964, 1967, and 1977). He was also a seven-time winner of the USAC championship (1960, 1961, 1963, 1964, 1967, 1975, and 1979).

From left to right, Mario Andretti and A. J. Foyt with fellow driver Bobby Unser in 1981. Tony Tomsic/Sports Illustrated/Getty Images

Hot-tempered outside a car, he was cool and determined behind the wheel.

Anthony Joseph Foyt, Jr., was born in Houston, Tex., on Jan. 16, 1935. When he was only four years old, his father, a garage owner and midget-car racer, built him a small gas-powered race car. At the age of 11, he began driving his father's midget cars. In 11th grade, he worked in his father's garage and raced professionally. His regular outfit of clean white trousers over cowboy boots earned him the nickname Fancy Pants. Foyt was a skilled mechanic, and early in his career he built many of his own cars.

Foyt first qualified for the Indianapolis 500 in 1958; the youngest driver in the race, he finished 16th. He won his first USAC championship in 1960 and his first Indianapolis 500 victory in 1961. The Auto Racing Fraternity of Greater New York named him Racing Driver of the Year in 1963. In January 1965, he was injured in a racing accident at Riverside, Calif. Nevertheless, he came back to win major races in Atlanta, Daytona Beach, and Trenton later that year. He won the Indianapolis 500 for the third time in May 1967, with an average speed of 151.207 miles (243 km) per hour.

Foyt competed successfully with stock cars, sprint cars, and midgets. He won the 1972 Daytona 500 and six other NASCAR races. In the 1980s, he won the Pocono 500, the Daytona 24-hour race (twice), and the Sebring 12-hour race. In 1989, he was in the first group inducted into the Motorsports Hall of Fame. He entered his last race in 1992 and retired in 1993. With Mario Andretti, Foyt was named Driver of the Century in 1999. He was inducted into the International Motorsports Hall of Fame in 2000.

JANET GUTHRIE

"In company with the first lady ever to qualify at Indianapolis — Gentlemen, start your engines." That statement began the 1977 Indianapolis 500, and the lady in question was the American race car driver Janet Guthrie.

Guthrie was born in Iowa City, Iowa, on March 7, 1938. Her father was an airline pilot, and by the age of 21 she could fly more than 20 types of aircraft. She received a bachelor's degree in physics from the University of Michigan and then worked as an aerospace engineer. In 1965 the National Aeronautics and Space Administration (NASA) considered making her an astronaut.

Janet Guthrie in 1980 at one of her final NASCAR races. **RacingOne/ ISC Archives/Getty Images**

Guthrie's competitive driving career began when in 1961 she entered gymkhana competitions, which require relatively low-speed, precision driving. She began high-speed racing in 1963. For nine straight times between 1964 and 1970, she finished in the top three American endurance races, winning two of them. When in 1976 lumber executive Rolla Vollstedt decided to sponsor the first woman in the Indianapolis 500, he chose Guthrie—but she failed to qualify because of engine limitations. For the rest of 1976 and in early 1977, she gained speedway experience in a series of top stock-car races, becoming in 1976 the first woman to compete in a NASCAR Winston Cup event.

Guthrie's official rookie season in NASCAR was 1977. She entered 19 races and qualified for all of them. She had a strong start, finishing 12th in the Daytona 500 on February 20, earning her the Top Rookie title. She earned the Top Rookie title again in the Richmond 400 a week later and four more Top Rookie titles by the end of the season. In her last race that year, she battled Bobby Allison, but engine failure forced her out of the race 25 laps before the finish.

In 1978, Guthrie completed the Indianapolis 500, coming in ninth in a field of 33. She also raced in the 1979 Indianapolis 500 but was unable to finish owing to mechanical problems. Having overcome both skepticism and on occasion outright hostility, Guthrie established herself as an outstanding professional race driver.

Guthrie's good showings at Indy and other tracks quieted traditionalists who discouraged woman racers. Although she continued to race into the 1980s, her career was stunted by a lack of funds. She was inducted into the Women's Sports Hall of Fame in 1980 and the International Motorsports Hall of Fame in 2006.

Junior Johnson

Junior Johnson ranks among the most influential figures in NASCAR history. One of NASCAR's most colorful characters, Johnson was a direct link back to the sport's early connection to liquor bootlegging. Though he never won a championship as a driver, he was an on-track innovator whose method of "drafting" changed racing forever.

Robert Glenn Johnson, Jr., was born on June 28, 1931, in Wilkes County, N.C. He grew up around both racing and illegal liquor running. He spent 11 months in prison for operating a liquor still, but he was never caught running moonshine. Spurred on by his experiences of eluding the police in North Carolina, Johnson began racing in the Grand National (now Sprint Cup) Series in 1955.

In 1960, Johnson discovered a racing technique that would transform the sport. While running in practice at Daytona International Speedway in Florida, he realized he could get in the slipstream of faster cars and keep up with them because of the vastly reduced wind resistance, a technique known as "drafting." With some skill, he could then slip out of the draft and pass the leading car, which was exactly what he did to win the Daytona 500 in 1960.

Johnson retired in 1966 with 50 Grand National wins, the winningest driver to have never won a championship, but he began a lucrative and heralded career as a stock-car owner. His drivers, including Darrell Waltrip and Cale Yarborough, brought him six NASCAR championships between 1966 and 1995, when he got out of the ownership game. Johnson was a member of the inaugural class of the NASCAR Hall of Fame in 2010.

David Pearson at the Daytona International Speedway in 1974. **Lane Stewart/Sports Illustrated/Getty Images**

DAVID PEARSON

David Pearson was one of the most successful drivers in NASCAR history. He could well have been the greatest NASCAR driver of all time had he competed in as many races as his rivals. He never raced a complete season schedule, but he still won three NASCAR championships (1966, 1968, and 1969), and his 105 wins over 27 seasons rank second only to Richard Petty's 200, even though he drove less than half as many races as Petty.

Born on Dec. 22, 1934, in Whitney, S.C., Pearson showed an interest in stock-car racing as a child. He started racing at dirt tracks at age 18 and in 1960 began racing in NASCAR's Grand National (now Sprint Cup) Series, earning Rookie of the Year honors.

Pearson won 3 of his 19 races in the next season. He would continue to race every year through 1986, notching at least one top-10 finish every year. His best years were 1966, when he won 15 races; 1968, when he won 16; and 1973, when he won 11 races while competing in only 18. In 1976, he won his only career Daytona 500.

Pearson and Petty formed NASCAR's most formidable rivalry. The two drivers finished first and second on 63 different occasions, with Pearson winning 33. Even Petty acknowledged that Pearson was not just his most fearsome competitor but quite possibly the best driver of all time.

When NASCAR announced its inaugural 2010 class of five inductees for its Hall of Fame, Pearson lost to Bill France Jr. by a single vote. He was overwhelmingly voted in the following year.

LEE PETTY

Lee Petty won the NASCAR championship three times in the 1950s. Although he is not as well-known as his son Richard, Lee deserves much of the credit for making NASCAR a national sport in the United States.

Lee Petty was born on March 14, 1914, in Randleman, N.C. Early in life he was a jack-of-all-trades: he farmed, drove everything from trucks to taxis, and repaired cars. He did not become involved in racing until 1949, when he heard that NASCAR was holding a race in Charlotte, N.C. He entered the family's car, a Buick, in the race and rolled the car four times.

The wreck only inspired Petty. He purchased a Plymouth and, with the help of his sons Richard and Maurice, began racing professionally. He went on to win three titles (1954, 1958, and 1959) and never finished lower than sixth in NASCAR's standings. His crowning year was 1959, a season that he began by winning the first Daytona 500. He

would go on to win 11 more races that season and the third of his three championships.

Two years later, during a qualifying race at Daytona, Petty's car collided with that of Johnny Beauchamp. The cars sailed together through a guard rail into the parking lot outside the track. Sustaining a head injury, a punctured lung, chest fractures, and multiple other injuries in the wreck, Petty was hospitalized for four months. His racing days were effectively over.

Petty won 54 races in 427 career starts in what is now NASCAR's Sprint Cup Series. He became a member of virtually every major racing hall of fame. In 1998, he was named one of NASCAR's 50 greatest drivers of all time, and in 2011 he was enshrined in the NASCAR Hall of Fame. He died in Greensboro, N.C., on April 5, 2000.

RICHARD PETTY

The first American race-car driver to earn more than $1 million in the sport was Richard Petty, who accomplished the feat in August 1971 and went on to total some $8 million for his career. Known as The King, Petty won seven NASCAR championships (1964, 1967,

Richard Petty is well-known outside of racing as well. He earned many young fans when he voiced "The King" in the Disney movie Cars. **Jon Kopaloff/FilmMagic/Getty Images**

1971, 1972, 1974, 1975, 1979), placed first at the Daytona 500 seven times (1964, 1966, 1971, 1973, 1974, 1979, 1981), and accumulated 200 first-place finishes.

Richard Lee Petty was born on July 2, 1937, in Randleman, N.C. His father, Lee, was a champion driver, and young Richard was often on Lee's crew. Richard started racing professionally at age 21, and by 1959 he was NASCAR's Rookie of the Year. His first win came in 1960 at the Charlotte Speedway in North Carolina.

Disputes over engine specifications led Petty to participate in a Chrysler boycott of NASCAR in 1965. He turned to drag racing, but tragedy struck when Petty's dragster went out of control and killed a boy in the stands. Petty later returned to NASCAR, having a remarkable year in 1967 with 27 wins (including ten in a row) and seven second-place finishes in 48 races. A very popular driver, he was often seen signing autographs at the track in his trademark cowboy hat and sunglasses.

The final win of Petty's career came on July 4, 1984, in the Firecracker 400 at the Daytona International Speedway in Florida. Petty's last race was in 1992 at the Atlanta Motor Speedway in Georgia.

Petty received NASCAR's Award of Excellence in 1987 and the United States Medal of Freedom in 1992. He was inducted into the International Motorsports Hall of Fame in 1997, and he was part of the inaugural class of the NASCAR Hall of Fame in 2010. His son Kyle and grandson Adam also raced in NASCAR series. In 2000, Adam Petty died in a crash during practice for the Busch Grand National at New Hampshire International Speedway.

CALE YARBOROUGH

Cale Yarborough was the first person to win the NASCAR championship in three consecutive years. He also won the Daytona 500 four times, placing him second behind Richard Petty's seven victories.

Cale Yarborough after his 1984 win in the Daytona 500. **Bob Harmeyer/ Archive Photos/Getty Images**

Cale Yarborough was born on March 27, 1939, in Timmonsville, S.C. He began driving stock cars in the early 1960s, and in 1968 he won four NASCAR races, including the Daytona 500; his three other wins at Daytona came in 1977, 1983, and 1984. After unsuccessfully driving USAC cars, he won his first NASCAR championship in 1976, repeating in 1977 and 1978. In 1977, he was the first NASCAR driver to start and finish 30 of 30 races. Yarborough retired in 1988. His autobiography, *Cale: The Hazardous Life and Times of America's Greatest Stock Car Driver,* appeared in 1986. Yarborough was inducted into the International Motorsports Hall of Fame in 1993 and the NASCAR Hall of Fame in 2012.

CHAPTER 4

CONTEMPORARY NASCAR STARS

As NASCAR has risen to an unprecedented level of popularity, its most successful and popular drivers have become household names. The drivers featured here are NASCAR legends in the making.

DALE EARNHARDT JR.

Dale Earnhardt Jr. was born to NASCAR royalty. He is the son of Dale Earnhardt, a seven-time Cup champion, and grandson of Ralph Earnhardt, the 1956 NASCAR Sportsman champion.

Dale Earnhardt Jr. was born in Kannapolis, N.C., on Oct. 10, 1974. His racing career began in the early 1990s mainly at the Myrtle Beach Speedway in South Carolina. Dale Sr. gave his 21-year-old son

Dale Earnhardt Sr. (left) *with Dale Earnhardt Jr. at the Bristol Motor Speedway.* George Tiedemann/Sports Illustrated/Getty Images

his first shot at the NASCAR Nationwide Series in 1996, where he finished an impressive 14th. The following year, Dale Jr. decided to skip going for Rookie of the Year and competed in eight races—one more than the maximum for rookie status. His best finish in 1997 was seventh. In 1998 he raced in all 31 Nationwide Series events and won the series title. He repeated as the series champion in 1999.

Earnhardt Jr. made his Sprint Cup debut in 1999 and joined the series full-time in 2000. His best season was 2004, when he finished with six wins, one of them in the Daytona 500. He raced to his second Daytona 500 win in 2014, at age 39. A fan favorite, he was selected as NASCAR's Most Popular Driver for 11 straight years beginning in 2003. He also has appeared numerous times in Harris Interactive's annual poll of the country's Top 10 Favorite Athletes. In 2012 his influence on and off the track earned him seventh place on *Forbes* magazine's list of Most Influential Athletes.

Earnhardt Jr. raced for his family's business, Dale Earnhardt, Inc., until 2008 when he made a switch to Hendrick Motorsports. The transition was covered by a five-part documentary series on ESPN called *Dale Jr.—Shifting Gears*. He also started his own company, JR Motorsports, which became one of the top organizations in the Nationwide Series.

JEFF GORDON

Jeff Gordon dominated NASCAR in the 1990s and early 2000s. His aggressive

Jeff Gordon waves to fans before a 2010 race at the Las Vegas Motor Speedway. Action Sports Photography/Shutterstock.com

driving style and knack for publicity helped popularize stock-car racing in the United States.

Gordon was born in Vallejo, Calif., on Aug. 4, 1971. As a child he raced BMX bicycles before being given a quarter-midget race car. He won the national quarter-midget championship at age eight and again two years later. When Gordon was 13, his family moved to Pittsboro, Ind., so that he could drive a 650-horsepower sprint car in races that did not have a minimum-age requirement. By the time he was 18, Gordon had decided to take up stock-car racing.

Gordon competed in NASCAR's Grand National Series (a level below Cup Series competition) before signing with Rick Hendrick, owner of a Cup Series team, in 1992. In 1993, Gordon earned Rookie of the Year honors. The following year he won the inaugural Brickyard 400, and in 1995 he claimed his first NASCAR championship. During the 1997 season, Gordon became the youngest driver to win the sport's premier event, the Daytona 500, and the first to win the Southern 500, NASCAR's oldest race, three times in a row. These victories helped him capture his second

NASCAR championship. In 1998, at age 27, Gordon tied Richard Petty's record of 13 victories in one season and became the youngest driver to win three NASCAR titles. He won his second Daytona 500 in 1999, and he took a fourth NASCAR championship in 2001. He won again at Daytona in 2005, though he finished that season 11th in NASCAR'S point standings, his lowest final ranking in 12 years.

Gordon returned to form in 2007, finishing second in that year's Cup standings. In 2008 and 2010, he posted zero Cup Series victories, but he still managed to garner enough points to finish in the top 10 of the standings each season. His four wins in 2014 were his highest total since 2007.

JIMMIE JOHNSON

Jimmie Johnson was the first race-car driver to win the NASCAR title in five consecutive years, from 2006 through 2010. He broke the 30-year-old record held by Cale Yarborough, who had captured three straight titles in the 1970s.

Jimmie Kenneth Johnson was born on Sept. 17, 1975, in El Cajon, Calif. He started competing in motor sports at age five and

Jimmie Johnson celebrates a win at the Texas Motor Speedway in 2012.
Beelde Photography/Shutterstock.com

won his first championship in motorcycle racing at eight years old. Eventually he turned to four-wheel vehicles and took up off-road racing, competing in leagues that included Short-Course Off-Road Drivers Association, SCORE International, and Mickey Thompson Entertainment Group. In 1998, he began to race in NASCAR's Busch Series, and by 2000 he was a member of Herzog Motorsports's Busch team, finishing third in that season's Rookie of the Year standings.

On Oct. 7, 2001, Johnson finished 39th of 43 drivers in his first appearance in NASCAR's Cup Series. He also earned his first Busch Series win in 2001, at Chicagoland Speedway, winding up eighth in the series' point standings. In 2002, he began his rookie season in the Cup Series, winning three races and ending the season ranked fifth. He finished second in the standings in 2003, with three victories, and did the same in 2004, when he won a series-best eight times. He finished fifth overall in 2005 before starting his dominant run the following season.

In 2006, when he won his first Cup Series championship, Johnson registered five victories, including the Daytona 500, and had 13 top-5 and 24 top-10 finishes. In 2007, he earned his second title, becoming the first driver to have 10 victories in a season. In 2008, Johnson won seven races and his third championship. In 2009, he captured his fourth title and was named Male Athlete of the Year by the Associated Press. Johnson's six victories in 2010 helped him secure a fifth championship.

Johnson's championship streak ended in 2011, when he finished the Cup Series season in sixth place, which he followed with a third-place finish in 2012. In 2013, he won his second career Daytona 500 title, and he finished that NASCAR season with his sixth career Cup Series championship.

DANICA PATRICK

Danica Patrick was the first woman to win an IndyCar championship event. She began racing in NASCAR events in 2010 and soon became one of the sport's most popular drivers.

Danica Sue Patrick was born in Beloit, Wis., on March 25, 1982. Her racing career began with go-karts in her hometown at age 10. At age 16, after national success in go-karts, Patrick left high school to race Formula Fords and Vauxhalls in the United

Danica Patrick won the Indy Japan 300 in 2008. She was the first woman to win an IndyCar race. AFP/Getty Images

Kingdom. She placed second in the 2000 Formula Ford festival, the best-ever finish for an American in that spawning ground for future professionals.

Patrick returned to the United States in 2002 after being signed to her first U.S. Indy-car racing contract by former Indy driver Bobby Rahal. She was then promoted to Toyota Formula Atlantic open-wheel cars. Although she never won in that series, she had a chance to qualify for the Indianapolis 500. Three other women—Janet Guthrie, Lyn St. James, and Sarah Fisher—had previously qualified for the Indy 500, the most prestigious auto race in the United States. In her first appearance at Indy, in 2005, Patrick set the fastest lap in practice (229.88 miles [370 km] per hour), but she could not duplicate this feat during official qualifying. She became the first woman to lead the classic race and eventually finished fourth. She was named Rookie of the Year for 2005 and was voted Indy Racing League (IRL) Most Popular Driver in 2005, 2006, and 2007.

Patrick began racing with the Andretti Green Racing (AGR) team in 2007. On April 20, 2008, in her 50th start in the IRL, Patrick secured the first big win of her career—the Firestone IndyCar 300 race at the Twin Ring Motegi circuit in Motegi, Japan. She finished 5.86 seconds ahead of former IRL titlist Hélio Castroneves of Brazil to become the first woman to win an IndyCar championship event.

Beginning in 2010, Patrick raced a partial season in NASCAR's lower-tier Nationwide Series in addition to continuing to compete in IndyCar racing. In August 2011, she announced that she would move to NASCAR full-time. Patrick won the pole position for the 2013 Daytona 500, becoming the first woman to start a Sprint Cup race from the pole. She also became the first woman to lead a lap in that race, and she finished in eighth place.

TONY STEWART

Tony Stewart is one of racing's most versatile drivers. He found success in both USAC and IndyCar racing before beginning his stellar NASCAR career.

Born on May 20, 1971, in Columbus, Ind., Stewart began racing go-karts in 1978. In 1980, at age eight, he won a four-cycle rookie junior class championship. This was followed by two national go-kart

Tony Stewart gets ready for a practice run at the Pocono Raceway on Aug. 2, 2014. **Chris Graythen/NASCAR/Getty Images**

championships. But he soon turned from go-karts to open-wheel machines, racing three-quarter midgets starting in 1989.

It was a sign of things to come when, in 1994, Stewart had five wins in 22 starts to take his first United States Auto Club (USAC) championship. This was followed by an incredible 1995 season, in which he became the first driver to win the USAC "Triple Crown"—the National Midget, Sprint, and Silver Crown championships. In 1996, he moved to IndyCar racing, entering the Indianapolis 500 and earning Rookie of the Year honors. In 1997, he won podium finishes in seven IndyCar events to capture the series championship.

Stewart made his NASCAR debut in the Nationwide Series in 1996. Three years later he moved to the Sprint Cup Series, winning three races and the Rookie of the Year award. He won his first Sprint Cup championship in 2002. His second title came in 2005, when he had five wins among his 17 top-five finishes. The 2011 season ended with Stewart tied in points with another driver, Carl Edwards. Stewart took the title in a tiebreaker, as he had five wins to Edwards' one.

Stewart went to great lengths to compete. In 1999, he competed in both the Indianapolis 500 and the Coca-Cola 600 on the same day, driving a total of 1,090 miles (1,754 km). In 2001, he did "double duty" again, driving a total of 1,100 miles (1,770 km) to break his own record for most miles raced in one day.

Tragedy struck on Aug. 9, 2014, when Stewart hit and killed a fellow driver, Kevin Ward Jr. following a crash that Ward had a few moments before. Ward was walking on the track when Stewart struck him. A grand jury declined to press criminal charges against Stewart. The incident prompted NASCAR to change the rules about driver conduct following an accident, stating that drivers must remain in their cars with their safety gear fastened until told to move by an official.

Whether you are sitting in the grandstands, holding binoculars as you follow your favorite driver around each lap, or sitting in your living room holding a bowl of popcorn and cheering as your driver moves forward to the next position, NASCAR is an exhilarating experience. For all ages, there is an intense thrill from watching skilled drivers race to the finish, risking life and limb in pursuit of the Cup.

NASCAR has been thrilling the country's racing fans for more than 60 years. From the very first bumpy races down the beach to the astonishing 200-mile (322-km) per-hour races around the world's best tracks, the sport keeps changing. But there is no doubt that one thing will stay the same: fans will keep watching, cheering, gasping, and loving every minute.

bootlegging Making or selling alcohol
  illegally.
circuit A series of sports events that are
  held or done at many different places.
dispute An argument or debate.
drafting The technique of staying close
  behind another racer to take advantage
  of the reduced air pressure created by the
  leading racer.
endurance The ability to do something dif-
  ficult for a long time.
enshrine To remember someone who is
  admired.
garner To acquire, collect, or earn.
go-kart A small car that has one or two
  seats and an open top and that is used
  especially for racing.
gymkhana A timed contest for automobiles
  featuring a series of events designed to
  test driving skill.
icon A widely known symbol.
inaugurate To be the beginning of something, such as a period of time.
jockeying Changing position in order to get
  an advantage.
lucrative Profitable.
midget A type of race car that is small, but
  has a high power-to-weight ratio.

midget car A miniature front-engine racing car.

open-wheel Describes a race car with its wheels situated outside of the main body of the car; sometimes called a formula car.

pole position The best position at the start of an automobile race.

preeminent Having the highest rank, dignity, or importance; supreme.

prestigious Respected; honored.

quarter-midget A type of racing car that is approximately one-quarter the size of a full-sized midget car.

restrictor plates A device installed in the intake of an engine that is designed to limit air flow and thereby limit the car's power.

sanction To officially accept or allow.

still An apparatus used in the distillation of liquor.

NASCAR
P.O. Box 2875
Daytona Beach, FL 32120
Website: http://www.nascar.com
The official site for NASCAR has news
    reports, race videos, track schedules,
    driver details, and much more.

NASCAR Foundation
One Daytona Boulevard, 6th Floor
Daytona Beach, FL 32114
(877) 515-4483
Website: http://www.nascarfoundation.org
The NASCAR Foundation supports a number
    of charities dedicated to helping children,
    with a special emphasis on education.

National Auto Sport Association
P.O. Box 2366
Napa Valley, CA 94558
(510) 232-6272
Website: http://www.nasaproracing.com
This organization is dedicated to organizing
    and promoting racing events throughout
    the country.

Sports Car Club of America (SCCA)
P.O. Box 19400

Topeka, KS 66619
(800) 770-2055
Website: http://www.scca.com
The SCCA offers its members opportu-
nities to get involved in motorsports
in a variety of ways. It provides staff
to NASCAR and other racing events
in areas including flagging and com-
munications, timing and scoring, and
emergency services.

Sportscar Vintage Racing Association
1598 Hart Street, Suite 100
Southlake, TX 76092
(817) 521-5158
Website: http://www.svra.com
This organization focuses on vintage racing,
sponsoring events featuring restored racing cars from the past.

Tony Stewart Foundation
5644 W. 74th Street
Indianapolis, IN 46278
(317) 299-6066
Website: http://www.tonystewartfoundation.org
This organization was started by
NASCAR driver Tony Stewart. It is
dedicated to raising funds to help care

for children diagnosed with critical or chronic illness, animals that are at-risk or endangered, and drivers injured in racing events.

WEBSITES

Because of the changing nature of Internet links, Rosen Publishing has developed an online list of websites related to the subject of this book. This site is updated regularly. Please use this link to access this list:

http://www.rosenlinks.com/SPOR/NASC

Bechtel, Mark. *He Crashed Me So I Crashed Him Back: The True Story of the Year the King, Jaws, Earnhardt, and the Rest of NASCAR's Feudin', Fightin' Good Ol' Boys Put Stock Car Racing on the Map.* New York, NY: Little, Brown and Company, 2010.

Bonsor, Kevin, and Karim Nice. "How NASCAR Safety Works." How Stuff Works. Retrieved August 4, 2014 (http://auto.howstuffworks.com/auto-racing/nascar/nascar-basics/nascar-safety.htm).

Edelstein, Robert. *NASCAR Legends: Memorable Men, Moments, and Machines in Racing History.* New York, NY: Overlook Press, 2012.

FactExpert. "NASCAR Racing Flags: Learning the Basics." Retrieved August 4, 2014 (http://nascar.factexpert.com/1225-nascar-flags.php).

Leslie-Pelecky, Diandra. *The Physics of NASCAR: The Science Behind the Speed.* New York, NY: Plume, 2009.

NASCAR. "NASCAR Sprint Cup." Retrieved August 4, 2014 (http://www.nascar.com/en_us/sprint-cup-series.html).

Page, Olivia. "What Are the Rules of Stock Car Racing?" How Stuff Works. Retrieved August 4, 2014 (http://auto.howstuffworks.com/auto-racing/nascar/nascar-basics/rules-of-stock-car-racing.htm).

Thompson, Neal. *Driving with the Devil: Southern Moonshine, Detroit Wheels, and the Birth of NASCAR*. New York, NY: Three Rivers Press, 2007.

White, Ben, and Nigel Kinrade. *NASCAR Then and Now*. Minneapolis, MN: Motorbooks, 2010.